THE
UNTENANTED ROOM

THE
UNTENANTED ROOM

Poem by James Simpson
Woodcuts by Carolyn Trant

With Best Wishes

James Simpson

AGENDA EDITIONS

First Published in 2011
by Agenda Editions
The Wheelwrights,
Fletching Street,
Mayfield,
East Sussex
TN20 6TL

Text copyright James Simpson 2011
Images copyright Carolyn Trant 2011
ISBN 978-0-902400-97-9

A CIP catalogue record for this book is available
from The British Library

Designed and typeset by Peter Flanagan
Printed and bound in Great Britain
by One Digital, Brighton

is supported by

for
Lindsay Clarke

I saw the forest and I saw the land;
I looked for marvels, but I could not find them.

Wace

I

We have come to this place
where we kill all gods and dreams,
something inconsequential
scribbled in the margin of our lives.

We write words, but words lie forgotten,
throats are cut, voices taken
and in a glance of life
we trample everything underfoot,
scrabbling to reach the chamber door.

Where oh where is the greenstick boy?
Who has heard the night bird's song?
Even the frosts are gone and the old grain
does not seem to grow anymore.

II

The bee is in the playground,
come down from the hill of neither mist nor rain:

she is sizeable; queen of a thousand worlds,
conjuring all the flowers from the meadow;

plantain and buttercup,
vetch's purple labia.

Have you walked this way
from the borders of the full sea;

your saffron hair with many tongues,
too many faces imploring God's pardon.

Have you passed this way before;
your arms like the burning

may blossom, crackling
blackthorn, sparks of elder.

A psalm for the plum's late bloom,
a psalm for the ivy flower's remaining sweetness;

a world of cares without understanding,
like a broken song thrush

whistling from its cardboard box;
punctured holes of light to sing for.

He killed the bee; no reason,
just out of place within these walls.

III

She learnt to hate
the blessed birds,
to save his heart from bird song.

At night whilst her son slept,
she would tear down
swallows' nests from under eaves;

sorting through the mud and straw
to find each egg
and best of all, those nestlings

who hadn't flown;
to squeeze their fragile heads between
her thumb and forefinger.

Every nest she ordered to be pulled down,
dove, and woodpecker,
thrush both missle and song.

Yet in the small hours she would lie awake,
waiting for the owls she loved,
listening to their soft calling.

IV

I covet the fire in him;
he is like spring light
on a winter bourne,
the first conjured sun.

Such beauty in the thundering hooves;
the fire, the fire,
shattering sparks,
struck from the forge.

To be him; like the great roar
of a yuletide burn,
like the beacon's flame
on the hill's back.

To be him.

Notice now the blood
hole in his chest,
my spear was always
an effective weapon.

Somehow he is dimmed:

It is as if he has walked too many miles
and the dust forms a lacquer on his hair;
eyes rimmed with salt,
paper thin, no tears left.

What is there to be said
about the awkward angle of his limbs,
as if his tripod has collapsed,
his hanging cage of ribs
rocking with the last sliver of breath.

What an audience he has.

V

Sift, sift my love
and take a snatch of honey
in your mouth.

The bees come to suckle you,
husk upon little husk,
it is a mean breath they offer.

Shh, there are no flowers
bless the rain on summer bowers,
let me tear each leaf in three

to twine around my fingers;
bind and unbind to find an end,
this the art to which I am given.

Lullay, lullay, my little liking,
let me cradle you in this shroud
like a leveret in his coffin.

VI

Gods lived here once
and men;
great works
scraped the sky
but the roofs fell in;
ripe skins burst
like a carcass bloated
in the sun;
even the flies have left
turned and run.

Gods lived here once
and men;
but the walls crumbled,
roads ruptured;
how quickly the gold lipped
turn grey;
broken into rubble heaps;
wall braces, iron piling
mangled, contorted to the abstract;

someone laughed here once
on this street corner;
saw the moon
in a pale day
and smiled;
all have passed away.

Here is the empty place,
the untenanted space
where no dweller dwells.
We are that place
not properly inhabited,
swept clean, adrift, cut off,
hung on the grid of numbers.

VII

A thin place in a thin time;
the blood bracked shuddering
in all the glass night;
and we the taut marchers and frost merriers

clasped onto earth's compass
and the crest capped haunches;
singing nights' crystal
and the ward welled blessing.

Through night's branches, gleaming
like starlings, over hillsides
and the breast papped chalk-lands,
lighted like candles and guttering torches.

Ours is the singing of the antlers blazing,
ours is the claim of the boar tusk whittling,
freeing the midden of the oak tree island,
singing the night and the unforgetting.

VIII

The sky is salt clear, a wave on ebbed air
bringing them in. Rook, jackdaw, ragged crow,
rising to their favoured place;
a single leafless tree:
                                    like a dressing of torn cloth.

He has no idea; walking blithely
through this world, the story seems lost to him.
Every step is a wound;
                                    how adept he is
in his own singularity.
Each crushing step; 'It's not me, It's not me.'

The tree draws them back;
                    throws them out again.

He gets up stunned;
                    the hammer blow of a beak
still echoing in his head.

                    Then the calls,
like women, like his mother, telling him
again and again.

Another smack;
like being slapped round the face;
                                    then another.

Clam breaker, nut cracker, cover your eyes.

He can feel the cool calm blood in his hair.
His arms are being pummelled, his fingers picked raw;

there are so many tearing at him now,
he has the taste of metal in his mouth.

He laughs at himself like one who knows
he is dying;

A chuckle.
              And for a moment the birds pause.

Swift, with all his reserve he
              slaps back a crow;
the bird wheels in the air,
              thuds to the ground,
a lame bundle.

The cawing stops.

            Only wind in the trees.

Before him a woman lies wounded;
her naked body curled like a shell.
He is on his knees.

            What has he done?

He has no idea.

IX

A dream I dream over:
like a fragment of touch
when a lover leaves for the last time;

hoping for a look back
down the hall. The hunted fox
heavy with cubs, run to distraction;

at last the supplicant, tongue lolling,
sitting, waiting, as the circle closes in.
Through the wood's bone cage,

through the orphaned trees,
stars seem like bare knuckles;
for she is gone, vixen to the night,

her cubs left mewling, blind.
Such a sudden birth;
the circle shrinks closes in.

Each cub, one by one,
lifted from the earth, their necks wrung;
but she is elsewhere, teats aching.

X

We could give you many heirs;
hanging from our black dugs
they would be worth a score
of thin boned progeny.

Such fine white throats we have
but we go by different names;
nettle creeper, hay sucker, muffit
and wheetie why; great peggy, meg cut throat.

You view us like a page from a newspaper:
what do you make of these photographs;
dead children wrapped in their mother's shawls,
picture on picture, death with no privacy?

Do you even ask the question?
Instead you fashion a shrunken world
where flickering screens survive
as some form of justification.

And in the end a lone white bear
is pawing the ocean, swimming in circles;
the last leaf of the arctic
drifting towards dark.

XI

There kneels God's knight,
his mind on other things:
blood specks the snow, a few

drops, the spoor of some dainty creature.
What is he looking at;
does he see something I do not?

One poor beast picked from the undulating line;
a clatter goose washed from the watery flood,
sunk far into the ocean streams

but raised living from the waves
by the air and wind,
carried far over the seal's back.

Such attention for a few drops of blood;
I was hanging out the washing;
hopeless really, no chance of anything

drying in such low cloud.
Then I heard them, the stubble geese;
a low clamour somewhere in the mist;

a growling chorus; many souls
talking at once; trying to say something;
but I could not understand what was missing.

XII

I have marked the dead seasons
one by one;
heard footfalls fall again,
fall in a night

so dark, that hills and sky
were one in sound
and still; but for the unusual air
twisting in the beech leaves.

What mysteries are these?
This mouthpiece uttering
the moon's limed walls.
Honest tongue,

there is nothing to be said:
this is the time of candle care
when frost lays
bitter the partial ground;

the lark has spun
the world on its axis;
and the blood
we have shed is mutual.

XIII

I do not know how to speak;
but dreams sift
into the waking mind,
intangible,

yet physical;
as the cuckoo's voice
somewhere in the goat willow.

Not there;
in the distance,
beyond earshot;

not there; out of reach,
inside the dream,
beyond the dream.

Passing away,
in the distance;
only a memory.
I do not know how to speak.

XIV

I have seen the battle of the years;
so I shall turn again into a hare
and shed my skin for this the final time.

The fields are silent, something is missing:
the corncrake in the pea-thistle,
the ebbing lapwing, the skylark's high fury.

Once a man talked of casting seeds;
but he is lost now
at the edge of understanding.

Let there be left a scatter of feathers
as when the fox carries off its prey:
a final moult to mark my dwelling place.

The world has had its play with me:
I shall lie low hidden in the earth's furrow;
until, until this time has had its lot with all.

James Simpson has collaborated with the artist and printmaker Carolyn Trant on the book Hunting the Wren (Parvenu/Actaeon Press). He recently won second prize in the Thomas Hardy Society's James Gibson Memorial Poetry Competition and has been anthologised in Our Common Ground (Silverdart Publishing), a collection of poems celebrating farming and the countryside. He has always lived in the South Downs and his work is deeply rooted in the area.

Carolyn Trant is an artist whose medium is Artists Books, taking a fresh look at myths and stories from popular culture, using her own texts or in collaboration with poets, such as David Harsent, Judith Kazantzis, Nicki Jackowska and James Simpson.

Her work is in private and public collections across Europe and the USA, including the British Library, Tate and V&A.